Beautiful
Colorado Country

"Learn about America in a beautiful way."

Beautiful
Colorado Country

Concept and Design: Robert D. Shangle
Text: Paul M. Lewis

Second Printing, October, 1982
Published by Beautiful America Publishing Company
P.O. Box 608, Beaverton, Oregon 97075
Robert D. Shangle, Publisher

Library of Congress Cataloging in Publication Data
Beautiful Colorado Country
1. Colorado—Description and travel—1951—Views. 1. Title.
F777.L48   917.88   80-18366
ISBN 0-89802-057-3
ISBN 0-89802-058-1 (hard)

Contents

Introduction

Nature has been so spendthrift in Colorado that to talk about the state is no easy matter. What to select for comment when there's so much to comment on? It's a big place, on the scale of the wide-open West around it. Only seven of the other 49 states are larger in area. Diversity is a key word for Colorado. So is livability. The high plains that underlie the Front-Range towns, where the majority of Coloradans live, are known far and wide for their comfortable and healthful climate.

Humidity can't amount to much because damp spots are hard to find. Water is the one gift that has not been given to Colorado in extravagant quantities. Outside of the mountains, the annual precipitation is positively meager. The San Luis Valley, midway along the southern border, has to make do with only seven inches annually. But to make up for the minimal rainfall on the flats, a vast treasure of moisture is stored on high, in the deep snows of the wide Rockies. The snow and ice of the mountains nourish the big rivers that pound down the east and west slopes and stretch like lifelines across the dry land. The big Colorado River starts small in Rocky Mountain National Park and gathers the waters of countless other streams along its westward course. One of those tributaries is the Gunnison, powerful canyon-cutter whose irrigation waters bring life to parts of the state's plateau country. The long and strong Arkansas River is born in the shadow of Mt. Elbert, Colorado's highest reach. The Arkansas turns the southeastern Colorado plains into a big fruit and vegetable garden. The South Platte heads northeast to the corner of the state. Its irrigated valley specializes in the growing of sugar beets. The Rio Grande rises in the San Juan Mountains and heads southeast around the edge of the high, dry San Luis Valley, where its waters are parceled out to widespread irrigation projects.

Colorado is the highest state, to be sure, but it has many levels, from 3,350 feet to beyond 14,000. Superlative settings are found at all elevations. They come in many shapes, materials, and colors. Canyons, mountains, broad valleys, mesas, and prairies are all represented. The rocks of the Rockies are of many varieties: limestones, marbles, granites, lavas, and sandstones. And a kind of mineral wealth never dreamed of by the first, frantic gold and silver prospectors is being extracted:

lead, zinc, copper, coal, petroleum, and natural gas. Add to that list some of the minerals essential to today's exotic technologies: uranium, vanadium, and molybdenum. So far, more than 3,000 species of flora have been identified in Colorado's five plant zones, from the plains to the alpine highlands. The animal communities on all of these levels also manifest a marvelous diversity.

So Colorado, with its variety of natural gifts, has been attracting many sorts of inhabitants for a long time. When the last glaciers retreated 10,000 or so years ago, the region became the home of several Indian cultures comprising plains, desert, and mountain tribes. Before the coming of the white man, the Cheyenne, Arapaho, Comanche, and Kiowa moved into the plains and plateaus, along with (to a lesser extent) Pawnee and Sioux. The Ute tribe, the only one indigenous to Colorado, ruled the mountain areas. Though the Indian inhabitants probably never numbered much more than 10,000, their tribal groupings represented different traditions and lifestyles, from the nomadic societies, who depended chiefly on hunting, to the farming tribes of the mesaland, who built permanent dwellings and practiced irrigated agriculture.

When man came in force, he represented even greater cultural disparity. The first great invasion—the ore hunters—was aptly characterized by Horace Greeley, during the Colorado segment of his trip across the country in 1859. Greeley sounds astonished as he records his impressions in his journal:

> Ex-editors, ex-printers, ex-clerks, ex-steamboat men . . . omnibus drivers from Broadway . . . ex-border ruffians from civilized Kansas. All of these, blended with veteran mountain men, Indians of all grades from the tamest to the wildest, half-breeds, French trappers and *voyageurs* . . . and an occasional Negro, compose a medley such as hardly another region can parallel. *

Men and women of different origins and viewpoints have continued to be drawn to Colorado from that day to this. The state's marvelous population mix may be, to some extent, responsible for the unusually mature outlook exhibited by Coloradans today. Amid the rush of modern life, they have paused to take stock.

Wilderness is unique, wilderness is fragile. Colorado has a lot of it left, and Coloradans seems to be of a mind to keep it from disappearing. We hope our book of Colorado landscapes will help to show people what is at stake.

P.M.L.

*Horace Greeley, *An Overland Journey*, ed. Charles T. Duncan, New York, 1964, p. 132.

Making the Scene

It used to be the gold and silver ores that attracted the multitudes to Colorado's Rockies. Miners are still digging into those hills, but these days the Shining Mountains are more beloved for their outside than for their inside. And some of the really big scenic shows of Colorado are in Rocky Mountain National Park, 405 square miles of very high and rugged mountain wilderness. The park is easy to reach from the cities of the Front Range. Denver, after all, is already a mile high. Estes Park is a convenient and popular gateway town next to the eastern park border. Estes Park has invented innumerable diversions for tourists, some of which have little to do with the Rocky Mountain region. Its views of big peaks are satisfying to those who are content to look at wilderness from afar and inviting to those who are not.

Trail Ridge Road provides the motorist with an easy way to see the park. Known as the longest high-mountain highway on the continent, it enters on the east at Estes Park and winds an erratic course across the park to the western side. The road then turns south to Grand Lake, two miles high on the southwestern park border. For 11 miles it swoops along above 11,000 feet, reaching a breathless high point in its northern course at 12,182 feet. At such elevations the world turns silent and watchful. The sky is a limitless well of intense blue; thousand-foot chasms drop away from the edge of the road down to forests, lakes, and glacial moraines. Powerful cataracts, fed by the everlasting snows of the Continental Divide, pound over deep clefts into dark canyons below. In summer the wind tundra crest line, at road level, glows with wildflower miniatures. Other life is present, too, at these heights. Marmots, pikas, and ptarmigans are sometimes seen. The immensity becomes intimacy when the mountains are explored on foot or horseback. The park has more than 200 pathways into back country inaccessible by other means. On the trail one is within arm's reach of everything, and the beauty of small natural forms brings delight. Wild creatures are abundant, and the hiker has the best chance of seeing them. The forests and mountain meadows are home to elk, deer, bighorn sheep, and birds in more than 200 assortments.

In western Colorado the mountains have subsided to more gentle crests and to high tablelands. The terrain turns upside-down in two remarkable examples of canyon-cutting by powerful rivers. The Dinosaur National Monument in the far northwest corner is one, and though overpowering in scale, its intricate canyons brilliantly illustrate the interplay of great and small in nature. The Yampa and Green rivers have cut a thousand feet into the plateau, and the steep walls are detailed in layered colors of endless variation. The sweep of the great chasms is observable from the rim. But closer study is also possible in guided trips on the rivers, riding a Navy neoprene landing craft that negotiates the white-water rapids with ease. Weird rock structures stand out from the cliffs, and hanging canyons astound the eye. For a more leisurely look, canyon explorers may hike along the bottom, where the rivers have left walking space. The name of Dinosaur has become somewhat misleading. Originally a smaller preserve was created to safeguard fossil dinosaur bones discovered there. Now protection is extended to all of the Green and Yampa river canyons.

Midway along the western border near Grand Junction, the Colorado National Monument takes in a climactic area of the high plateau. Canyons, escarpments, and brute-sized pillars of varicolored sandstone spread over the mesaland. Flat-topped mountains raise white or deep-red walls with sudden authority over a vast sage brush plain, where the big Colorado River seems shrunken to a trickle. Grand Mesa, the largest of the tablelands, rises 10,500 feet from cliffs above the river valley. Grand Mesa carries a spacious assortment of lakes, deep green forests, waterfalls, and canyons on its immense back.

Another brawny western-slope river flows through the broad plateau country. The Gunnison joins the Colorado at Grand Junction, after flowing through the Black Canyon of the Gunnison National Monument upstream near Montrose. The gorge is aptly named, so narrow that it is lighted only briefly by the noonday sun. At other times the ten-mile-long gorge is lost in deep shadow. The Black Canyon is in one of the wilder corners of Colorado, but there are several ways to explore its dark beauty. By car, from the rim drive, is one. Still better is the trail along the north rim, because it reaches the narrowest point, where the canyon is only 1,300 feet across. The shivery thrill of standing on the brink of a 2,800-foot deep river canyon is intensified by the narrow opening. The most persistent, or adventurous, or foolhardy visitors are the ones who creep down the nearly vertical sides to investigate the dark floor and the river itself.

Mesa Verde does a double number, refreshing your sense of history and stirring your esthetic pleasure. The preserve, one of Colorado's two national parks, covers 80 square miles of southwestern Colorado tableland and hilly, wooded areas of juniper forests and sandstone high above Montezuma Valley. The history lesson is in the form of the remarkably well-preserved Indian cliff dwellings, which are the principal feature of the park. Known as Balcony House, Cliff Palace, Spruce Tree House, and Square Tower House, these apartments in stone were occupied by the Basket Weavers and later the Pueblo Indians of the Anasazi culture. The Anasazi (Ancient Ones) lived in west and northwest Colorado for some 1,300 years. Their disappearance was sudden, and historians believe they moved on after a series of drought years in the latter part of the 13th century, hurried on their way by the raids of hostile Navajos and Apaches.

It would seem unlikely that the largest sand dune formations occur in Colorado, an inland state. But the folks who set up the Great Sand Dune National Monument were not being hoaxed by a mirage. There they are, just under the western slope of the Sangre de Cristo Range, undulating over the San Luis Valley for 57 square miles. What created these great sand hills? Three major elements are involved: the dry, sandy floor of the San Luis Valley, the prevailing southwest winds, and the Sangre de Cristo Range. The winds pick up the sand and drop it at the base of the mountains. This has been going on for a long time, and the ever-growing dunes now reach as high as 600 feet. With the flutings, swirls, and ripples characteristic of sand dunes, they flow over the valley floor, resembling graceful specters in the morning light over the Sangre de Cristos. The natives are known to tell eerie tales to travelers, of ghostly herds of sheep and horses haunting the sands during the darkest hours.

Colorado's natural extravaganzas dominate by the sheer power of their presence. The breathtaking mountain uprushes, the mysterious dark corridors of river canyons, the fast-flowing rivers and streams, and the endless prairies owe a part of their glamor to the smaller components of the scene, the wildflowers. They are the icing on the cake, blooming in spring and summer in mountain glades, on canyon walls, along stream banks, and in waving masses on the open plains.

All over Colorado flowering plants, ferns, shrubs, and grasses appear in myriad forms and colors. With five plant zones, the variations are endless. On the prairies alone are some 500 kinds of plant life. The cactus comes in 25 varieties. Among the spring flowers of the prairie are the sand lily; the evening primrose, in cream or rose pink; the coral-colored wild geranium; the buttercup, and the white star flower. The hotter-weather kinds, like the sunflower, the purple-tasseled scotch thistle, and loco weed, bloom up to midsummer. In the most arid parts of the plains, we find the cockleburr, silvery sage, mesquite shrub, and the yucca plant, put to so many uses by the Indians.

The lower slopes are home to Indian paint brush, woods violets, blue bells, wild roses, Mariposa lilies, brown-eyed Susan, and mountain daisy. In the high valleys and along streams are lady slipper, calypso, and lady's tresses. In summer, the high mountain meadows are covered in lavish yellow with alpine gold-flowers. Keeping them company are the purple anemone, the white marsh marigold, and the alpine primrose. Individually these small residents of the plains, forests, or mountain meadows are shy and retiring, but being sociable, they usually prefer to live with many others of their kind. In their multitudes they bring a dimension of beauty and mystery to the scene that would not be there without them.

Mountains, Parks, and Plains

The major mountain groupings of Colorado's Rockies are not so much ranges as great, irregular ridges with high valleys or ''parks'' in the spaces between them. Their separation and differences in formation, however, allow distinctive labels to be given them. The Front, Park, and Sawatch ranges are closely grouped in a north-south direction. They wall in a high valley that extends north into Wyoming and south to the Sangre de Cristo Mountains. This intermontane area is divided into three distinct basins called parks—North, Middle, and South. They contain the headwaters of major rivers: the Platte in North Park, the Colorado in Middle Park, and the South Platte in South Park. These high meadowlands have relatively stable temperatures and moderate precipitation, protected as they are by the mountains around them. A fourth such park is the San Luis Valley, between the Sangre de Cristo Range in south-central Colorado, and the San Juan Mountains in the southwestern region.

For most Coloradans, the Rockies are the Front Range, because they are closest to the big towns. The eastern wall extends from the Laramie Range in Wyoming to the Colorado Springs area. Up and down that line are hundreds of giants 14,000 feet tall or better, topped by Longs Peak at 14,256. Longs is one of the select number of peaks that pose a serious challenge to climbers. Its east face, the Diamond, is straight up and down for 1,700 feet. More widely known than Longs, but no climber's mountain, is majestic Pikes Peak, rising from the plains at the southern end of the range. It's a respectable 14,110 feet, and its separation from other mountains gives it a commanding appearance. The peak is named after an Army lieutenant with the musical name of Zebulon Montgomery Pike, who is credited with its ''discovery.'' The quotes around that word are in respect to both the Spanish, who claim to have seen it first, and the Indians, who were around before anyone else. Pike came to the mountain when he was exploring the Louisiana Purchase, in 1806, for the United States government. Traveling up the Arkansas River, he eventually reached the peak that was to bear his name.

Pikes Peak overlooks the Garden of the Gods, a grouping of red sandstone pinnacles that rise from the valley floor like offshoots of the big mountain. The Flatirons, up north at Boulder, are a related phenomenon.

The Sawatch and Park ranges form the long western wall of the parks, or high valleys, between them and the Front Range. The Sawatch is associated with many of the gold and silver bonanzas of 1860 and 1877, and includes Mt. Elbert, highest of the Rockies at 14,433 feet. Nearby, and nearly as high, is Mt. Massive, silver ore repository and backdrop for the mining town of Leadville.

Two rugged and remote mountain blocks dominate the southern high country. The Sangre de Cristo chain of the south-central region reaches over the line into New Mexico, forming the southern end of the Rockies. Early Spanish padres get credit for the name, presumably an outcome of their first sight of the red-rock mountains. They had come upon them in the late afternoon, when the setting sun had turned the peaks a glowing reddish-purple: *Sangre de Cristo*—Christ's Blood. Under such light the intensity of the colors is accentuated by the sharpness of the crest and the fold lines.

The San Juan Mountains have staked out the southwest, across the broad San Luis Valley from the Sangre de Cristo Range. They are much more irregular in form than the other Colorado ranges and represent many different groupings, among them the La Plata, San Miguel, Needles, and Sneffels formations. Within a few miles of Durango, the big town in these parts, the high wilderness beckons with the lure of fishing, hunting, skiing, and exploring.

The Great Plains

A third of Colorado has no mountains at all. East of the Rockies is Colorado's share of the northern and southern Great Plains, that high and dry swath that cuts through the middle of the United States. Many visitors, motorists especially, can't wait to put them behind, to get to the "pretty part," where the mountains begin. And they miss a lot of satisfaction by not doing more pausing and looking. This empty land is no longer as empty as it was a hundred years ago.

In our day the prairie land has lost some of its open and trackless mystery. But there is still a feeling of spaciousness and solitude in what has become farming country on a grand scale. The stretches of desolation are now broad carpets of alfalfa and hay, oceans of wheat and corn. In some areas farmers have forced the soil to cooperate by bringing in water from the Rockies or tapping underground sources.

The high plains are fertile enough, built up millions of years ago by deposition from the Rockies' streams and by glacial loess left behind after the last Ice Age.

The human population is still thin. One may drive for miles over flat or gently rolling prairie without seeing another car, another person, or even a house. Reminders of human occupancy may be only the roadside telephone poles and occasional cultivated fields dotting the open land. In the north, east of the town of Sterling, this is the look of things. Here, also, is most of the dry farming potential of eastern Colorado. Dry farming is a technique that takes advantage of the low annual rainfall and of underground water, while adopting practices that conserve moisture.

Farther west, the lower valley of the South Platte runs through the northern plains, growing the crops that prefer wet to dry. Rolling hills and lowlands support lush farms irrigated by river water. This valley grows more sugar beets than any other area in the country, drawing migrant workers of varied ethnic backgrounds from Colorado's cosmopolitan population. Growing sugar beets used to mean a lot of hand labor. Now tractor-drawn machines do the uprooting and topping. The beets are processed in several towns along the river, including Sterling, which is the biggest (about 10,600).

East-central Colorado is, if anything, even more arid. The open grasslands are to the liking of antelope herds. And dry farmers make a living here, too. Wheat and corn are grown in scattered locations, where some irrigation water is available. So, too, are oats, rye, beans, and barley. Farther south, along the route now known as US 40, pioneer wagon trains got their first glimpse of the Shining Mountains as they left the stage stop of Cheyenne Wells on their way to Kit Carson. In the 1850s and 60s, the dry, open land took its toll of the multitudes trekking west to the gold fields. Especially during the ill-fated Pikes Peak Gold Rush of 1859, many inexperienced fortune-hunters died of hunger and thirst trying to cross over this part of Colorado. And some perished at the hands of Indians, enraged at the invasion of their buffalo hunting grounds.

Memories of wagon trains, frontiersmen, outlaws, and Indian troubles are deeply etched into the pattern of life of Arkansas River valley towns in the southeast. The Madonna of the Trail monument in Lamar honors the courageous mothers who helped keep the covered wagons moving along the Santa Fe Trail. Las Animas has the Kit Carson Museum, housing mementos of the famous hunter and trapper. Between that town and La Junta on the west is the site of Bent's Fort, the rest stop on the trail that was also a trading post and dispenser of a potent whiskey known as Taos Lightning. The Indians hung around to do some bartering with the assorted types passing

13

through on their way to someplace else. Chivington, up in the sagebrush country north of the big river, is named for Col. John M. Chivington, who, on November 29, 1864, led a bloody raid by his territorial troops on an Indian village at nearby Sand Creek. The affair subsequently became notorious as the Sand Creek Massacre and aroused a nationwide furor.

The fertile Arkansas River valley has become one of the country's big producers of vegetables and melons. The agricultural emphasis has largely replaced once-vast cattle grazing operations. In Rocky Ford, west of La Junta, the big business is the growing of vegetables and flowers for seed. A lot of backyard botanical miracles around the country were conceived in the seed plants of southeastern Colorado. Still farther south, in the very corner of the state, the grasslands have been largely reclaimed from the fearful ''Dust Bowl'' days of the early 1930s. Increased rainfall and more careful ''desert farming'' have brought the land back to life. Recovery has been slow, and whirling dust is still a threat when the wind gets a notion.

The People Places

Colorado is still one of the empty spaces, although its population is now something more than the 2,207,000 counted in the 1970 census. Maybe that figure doesn't seem like a lot of individuals in a nation of 215 million. But if you ever tried to count to a million by ones, that many of something makes a big impression. By far, most Coloradans live in the line of cities snuggled up to the Front Range. Greater Denver alone is a million and a quarter strong; Colorado Springs adds another 140,000 and Pueblo more than 100,000. Ft. Collins, Loveland, Greeley, Longmont, Boulder, and smaller places up and down the line add up to about 250,000 more. That leaves the rest of Colorado's 103,948 square miles to the equivalent of a dozen or so good football crowds.

The capital city, Denver, sprawls over a mile-high plain next door to the Front Range. The oasis where Denver began its career is watered by Cherry Creek, flowing northwestward, and the South Platte River, which runs northeast. The site at the confluence of the two streams had been used as a meeting place by the Cheyenne and Arapahoe, long before the white man became interested in it. Denver is supposed to have been founded on a "jumped claim." The record does show that a group of opportunists headed by William H. Larimer of Leavenworth simply confiscated claims previously staked out on the north and south banks of the two streams by speculators with future gold strikes in mind. Larimer named his town for Kansas territorial governor James W. Denver, unaware that Denver was no longer in office and so unable to do Larimer any favors.

Denver's shaky start didn't hold it back. It beat out other towns of the high plains, supposedly better situated for commerce or agriculture, to become Queen City of the Plains. Today, Denver is a mixture of sophistication and innovation. Even if it weren't on the front door of the Rockies, it would be a popular travelers' destination in its own right. It is certainly a good place to live and work, with a diversity of opportunity. A wide range of highly specialized industries have moved in. Aerospace, for one. So, too, have many federal agencies, so many that Denver is becoming an annex to Washington, D.C. All this has raised the percentage of scientists and

specialists in residence to the highest of any community in the nation. Denver University, the Colorado School of Mines, and the University of Colorado at nearby Boulder do their share to nourish the intellectual and creative atmosphere.

A well-founded Denver boast has to do with climate. Colorado is an inland state, with no water of any significance outside of that stored in the mountains as snow and ice. So Denver is high and dry. Even if the weather gets very hot or very cold and snowy for short spells, the low humidity keeps the comfort quotient high. Undeniably, to live in Denver is to be a lover of mountains. Which is not to say that all Denverites spend their leisure hours gallivanting among the glaciers and forests of the high country. The Rockies are simply there, and that's enough for some city dwellers who have yet to set foot on a mountain trail. On the other hand a great many others do join their brethren from different east-slope towns for vacations and weekends in the Rockies. They do what most people do in the scenic places of the West—take the well-trodden pathways into the organized playgrounds on the fringes of the wilderness.

Denver's past, from the ''jumped-claim'' beginnings to the present, has been crowded with events of great moment, such as gold fever, Indian conflicts, the flooding of Cherry Creek, and fires. But the city grew steadily after the chaotic gold-hunting period, in spite of catastrophe and isolation. Today Denver's cultural and historical concerns are well represented by outstanding museums and galleries. Among these are the Denver Art Museum, the Colorado State Historical Museum, and the Denver Museum of Natural History, all in the company of the finest institutions of their kind.

A settlement, which never really made it, was founded in 1859 along Fountain Creek where the ''Old Town'' part of Colorado Springs now stands. Its promoters hoped to attract people by billing it as the gateway to the gold riches in South Park, the broad mountain valley that extends south and west of the Front Range. South Park's treasure turned out to be a little less than lavish, and the village, known first as El Dorado City, then as Colorado City, would have become a ghost town except for being handy as a refuge for miners and cattlemen when the Ute Indians got riled up. About a decade later, the real ''gold'' was discovered when a new Colorado Springs was laid out to the east at the instigation of railroad promoter William J. Palmer, who saw the resort potential of the magnificent site.

The beautiful setting of Colorado Springs is nature's contribution. The town lies near the base of Pikes Peak on a gently rolling plain, with forested foothills and canyons between it and the mountain. The town itself is man's contribution, tailored

Horn Peak in the Sangre de Cristos

View from Wolf Creek Pass near Pagosa Springs

Mt. Meeker, Rocky Mountain National Park

19

Alta Mine

San Juan Range in the Rockies

Buffalo farm near Gunnison

Cliff Palace at Mesa Verde National Park
(Following pages) Rail fence in the Sneffels Range

Yampa River, Dinosaur National Monument

White River National Forest
(Preceding page) Trappers Lake near Buford
(Second preceding page) Arapaho National Forest

29

The Rocky Mountains

Boulder Brook, Rocky Mountain National Park

Dinosaur National Monument

The Sneffels Range near Ridgeway

33

Sheep grazing in the San Juan Rockies

The Sneffels Range

White River National Forest

The "Lost Horse Mill" along the Crystal River

Woods Lake in the San Juan Rockies
(Following pages) Wilson Peak

Cattle grazing in the Sangre de Cristo Mountains

39

Twin Sisters, Rocky Mountain National Park

Windmill on plains east of Colorado Springs

Bear Lake, Rocky Mountain National Park

The Rocky Mountains in autumn

Colorado National Monument

Pawnee Buttes, Pawnee National Grasslands

47

Bear Lake and Hallett Peak

Autumn in the San Juan Rockies near Dunton

48

Cabin in the Rockies
(Preceding page) Black Canyon, Gunnison National Monument
(Second preceding page) White River National Forest

Long's Peak in the Rocky Mountain National Park

Abandoned mine above Leadville

North Fork of the White River near Buford
(Following pages) Maroon Lake and Bells

Old mine near Lake City
(Preceding page) Meadow near Telluride
(Second preceding page) Primrose and marigolds in the Front Range

Ghost town of St. Elmo in the Rockies

Rocky Mountain National Park

Abandoned ranch near Telluride

63

with flair and taste into a resort community of extraordinary charm. In the century since Colorado Springs was founded, it has become one of the nation's solid tourist attractions. Called simply ''The Springs'' by Coloradans, it is 55 miles down Interstate Highway 25 from Denver. No small part of its attraction derives from a climate that is superb throughout the year. The community was leisure-oriented from the start, a place where persons of wealth retired to build their fine manors in the continental manner. It has mineral springs, too, in close-by Manitou Springs, which lends its healing waters in addition to part of its name to its snazzy neighbor. Colorado Springs has little industry outside of the tourist variety, so that there's nothing much around to tarnish its squeaky-clean air. It seems appropriate that the Garden of the Gods is in the Colorado Springs neighborhood. The ridges of grotesque red rock sculptures seem to be manifestations of nature's creativity.

Creative living of a more day-to-day kind is offered by the town at the southern end of the Front Range. Pueblo was built on industry, notably on steel manufacturing. The chief employer there is still a steel mill, one that fired up in 1881 and grew with the town. Pueblo's Spanish name fits very well. The site was an advance post of the 17th-century Spanish explorers, and today the most numerous of its several ethnic populations are the Spanish Americans. In the early days, the steel mills attracted workers of many nationalities—Spanish, Italians, Germans, Poles, Scandinavians, Slovaks, and more. Now a diversified industrial base, including agriculture, helps keep them here.

As a truly cosmopolitan city, Pueblo has avoided areas of wealth and poverty, giving it a kind of livability that would be the envy of places similar to it in size. There is also the built-in livability characteristic of Front-Range towns. The mountains are not quite as close as they are to Denver or Colorado Springs. This being so, Pueblo's air doesn't get backed up against them, with the resulting atmospheric stagnation. Pueblo boosters take advantage of this situation to point out that their town's air quality is even better than that of the other two cities. And they have the figures to back it up. There is lots of water on the immediate premises, too. The mighty Arkansas River flows through town from west to east in the early stages of its 2,000-mile journey to the Mississippi River. Fountain Creek comes in from the north. Backed up into a reservoir, the river supplies abundant water to keep Pueblo growing, slow and steady, for many years to come.

Pueblo and Colorado Springs both have a lead on other Front-Range towns in another way. They have easy access to some wild and gorgeous mountain, canyon, and mining country. The Arkansas River's Royal Gorge is just a 39-mile drive west

Log cabin in the Rockies near Silverton

of Pueblo on a good road. If not one of the deepest canyons, it's assuredly one of the steepest.

Famous old Cripple Creek lies in the hills a little west of Colorado Springs. The last and richest of the gold mining districts, it was born in the early 1890s when the silver boom had shrunk to a pop. Cripple Creek and nearby Victor were jammed with 20,000 inhabitants in their heyday. The mines yielded 15 million dollars a year in gold ore for a decade. More than 300 million dollars worth has been dug out of the hillsides to date. Cripple Creek's long-sustained riches gave it a free-wheeling, Wild West flavor around the turn of the century. The main non-mining activity was gambling. The most numerous buildings were saloons, dance halls, bawdy houses, and tents, from which miners could be outfitted with practically anything necessary and unnecessary for their prospecting.

When the glory days were finally over, Cripple Creek faded, almost, to a ghost town, but it now has a second life as a thriving tourist stop.

Central City is another gold camp that made it as a tourist attraction after running out of ore. It is a monument to the first great gold-inspired stampede into Colorado in 1859, the one grown famous for the ''Pikes Peak or Bust'' slogan, which symbolized the misdirected efforts of many untrained prospectors. The Pikes Peak area was indeed a bust for those who headed in that direction. But the steep gulch, a few miles west of Denver where Central City grew up, was for real. Colorado's first big gold strike was made there. It turned out to be a gold mine, so to speak, for one John H. Gregory. Gregory's undying determination, persistence, and hard work finally made him wealthy. From his vein of lode gold and others established in ''Gregory's Gulch,'' about 85 million dollars in ore was extracted. Gregory was a hard-bitten mountain man who worked alone. He resented the ''trespassers'' who swarmed into the gulch after his find was reported, reaping the fruits of his patient, difficult search. But his resentment stopped short of the dollar, and he made a fortune by selling rights to his original mine and others in the area. ''Green'' Russell, a gold prospector from Georgia, who had traveled over much of the Rockies with his party looking for the precious ore, established a claim in a nearby area, later named Russell Gulch. His find was even richer than Gregory's original one. Russell, a cosmopolitan, educated man in marked contrast to Gregory, was just as rugged and determined. His interests extended beyond the hunt for gold. Russell's land speculations in this area involved him in the founding of the nearby community of Aurora, ''twin'' of Denver City.

Two well-known eastern journalists, Horace Greeley and Henry Villard, helped swell the rush to the gold fields. Their reports, though cautious, fostered the legend about the bonanza lying there for the taking in Colorado Territory. The first person to flash the story of Gregory's gold was William N. Byers in his *Rocky Mountain News*. He beat the opposition to the streets in Denver with the news on May 28, 1859. Byers is one of the big names in Colorado affairs of this period. His newspaper is, today, one of the West's most distinguished. Byers, through the *News*, promoted Denver City and the young Colorado Territory as desirable places for settlement. He used gold fever to further this idea, taking visiting newspapermen, like Henry Villard, in charge when they came to inspect the Gregory Gulch operation.

Blackhawk, where mills and smelters were built, is next door to Central City. Together, the two relics of the golden days draw many thousands of visitors, during the season, to their high mountain environs where 15,000 persons once lived. A good deal of gold-camp nostalgia is still there. Victorian homes of some original residents hang onto the steep hillsides. The Central City Opera House goes on, well-built evidence of the town's early love for the theater and opera. Today it is often the setting for concerts and plays featuring the country's leading artists. The Teller House, built in 1872, and a very posh place in its time, still fulfills its original mission as a bar and hotel. The famous *Face on the Barroom Floor* was painted there by artist Herndon David in 1936 as a prank. Abandoned mining sites nearby can be visited, too. Russell Gulch, for instance, is reached by a road from town. Central City is 8,500 feet up in the mountains, and travelers get to see some of the awesome scenery that gold miners were too busy to make a fuss over. The short trip to Idaho Springs is a fall season spectacular, with the gold of aspen leaves.

Leadville is as famous for silver as Central City is for gold. Fabulous gold strikes were made here, too, but when the gold deposits were played out, the silver discoveries brought even greater riches. Leadville is associated with H.A.W. Tabor, the most famous personality of Colorado's silver boom. Tabor arrived in Colorado from his native Vermont in 1859. He had no money and didn't improve his lot very much during many years of drifting from gold field to gold field. But in Oro City, later to be incorporated as Leadville, he invested 17 dollars in grubstaking two silver prospectors. This was the beginning of his celebrity as Colorado's Silver King. The man immediately struck a phenomenal silver vein, and after a year, Tabor was able to sell his share in the mine for one million dollars. He then reinvested the money in even bigger enterprises, including what has become one of the most celebrated silver mines in the world—the Matchless. It was probably the most profitable of the mines he sank himself, yielding $100,000 a month. When Leadville was incorporated in 1878, Tabor became mayor and postmaster. The silver magnate of ''Cloud City'' (Leadville is nearly two miles above sea level) now operated several mines and sold supplies to silver miners. Having amassed a fortune of around ten million dollars, he divorced his wife, Augusta, married his mistress, Baby Doe, built an opulent opera house in Leadville, a more opulent one in Denver (in 1881), and other big buildings in both towns. He even served as an interim United States senator for a brief time (Colorado became a state in 1876). Tabor's showy style of life and the eventual collapse of the silver market left him penniless before his life was ended.

The San Juan Mountains spawned their share of gold and silver cities in this southwest part of Colorado. Two well-known communities, which have taken up new and successful careers, are Ouray and Telluride. The 1880s were the boomtown days for them. Now their primary treasure is in the year-round outdoor recreation they offer in the matchless San Juans, most especially skiing.

Mining still goes on at some Ouray diggings. The Camp Bird Mine of Thomas Walsh is one. Camp Bird was the biggest producer in the area, yielding four million dollars a year in gold for awhile. Walsh's daughter, Evelyn Walsh McLean, later became famous as the owner of the ''Hope Diamond'' and as a figure in Washington society. Ghostly remains of the mining heyday haunt the mountain slopes and valleys around Ouray. Ruined buildings bear witness to former towns, and headframes mark old mines.

Ouray is 7,800 feet up in a high mountain valley drained by the Uncompahgre River. Steep canyon walls hem in the town on three sides, giving it a ''made in Switzerland'' look. From the high ground an array of peaks can be seen in the surrounding near distance. One is Mt. Sneffels, 14,143 feet, rising to the west across the high Uncompahgre Plateau's pine forests and sagebrush plains. The pines of the plateau are accompanied by platoons of quaking aspen, those quivery-leafed trees that seem to tremble when one looks at them. The aspens not only quake, they glow with a brilliant fire against the somber pines when the first frosts touch their foliage.

Over the hill and not far away is Telluride. It's a little place that's rather big on the wild and free-swinging style of its 1890s mining boom. Designated a National Historic Landmark, the town looks like a memento of the past with its many old-time bars, an opera house, and other Victorian buildings. A number of notorious characters are part of its past. Butch Cassidy, the likeable cattle rustler and bank robber, once withdrew all the money from the town bank without benefit of an account. Telluride still has its characters, some of whom may be famous, but never infamous. Telluride is high up in San Juan ski country, upholstered with slopes that make the sport a major attraction.

The mining communities were generally placid towns. Though all the diversions were provided, many of the miners brought their families as soon as they could, and lived sober lives, in every sense of the word. Apparently their single-minded devotion to a goal kept them on the straight and narrow path. But one of the richest of the silver-era camps departed from the norm. Creede, on the high eastern slopes of the San Juans, became an instant town by the upper Rio Grande River when Nicholas C. Creede struck a silver vein there in 1890, said "Holy Moses!" and established his mine of the same name. Other big strikes in the area brought the town's population to 8,000 by 1893. Gunfights, gambling, and prostitution were a way of life in Creede during the silver bonanza days.

Across the Continental Divide from Leadville is another isolated mountain town that made a career out of silver mining, then turned into one of the world's premier ski resorts. As if that weren't enough, Aspen has become a cultural mecca too, attracting students from far and wide to its humanities and music studies. The mountains, which cut it off from the rest of the world, also provide the long and rigorous ski trails in the winter and the forests, lakes, and streams that make it such a choice setting for summer students. Over the mountains to the northeast is Vail, a close rival for the affections of skiers. Vail is the latest of the big-time resorts tailored to the business of downhill racing.

One of the wooliest of Colorado's wild 1880s towns is in the southwest corner. Durango does very well these days as the trade and tourist center of the area. Well situated in the San Juan basin near the Four Corners Indian Reservation country, Durango makes a living from the Animas River farmlands and from the range lands spread over the high plateau farther west. The shoot-'em-up scenario may no longer be Durango's thing, but the town still has the look and flavor of the brawling frontier days. One piece of nostalgia is the narrow-gauge Rio Grande line from Durango to Silverton. Daily, during the summer, a train of antique coaches crowded with railroad buffs and tourists, and pulled by a chugging steam engine or two, snakes up the steep Animas River canyon to the mining town 9,318 feet up in the mountains. This is one of the few remaining branches of the rail lines that were built to carry ore during the silver boom times. The excursion train returns to Durango in the afternoon, after the passengers have had a chance to visit in Silverton, looking into souvenir shops and abandoned buildings, visiting the museum in the Grand Imperial Hotel, and otherwise getting the feel of one of the legendary mining communities.

Photo Credits

JAMES ADAMS—*page 17.*

GENE AHRENS—*page 47.*

JAMES BLANK—*page 19; page 20; page 22; pages 24-25; page 27; page 29; page 32; page 33; page 34; page 35; page 36; page 37; page 38; page 39; page 43; page 44; page 46; page 48; page 49; page 51; page 52; page 53; page 54; page 55; page 59; page 60;page 61; page 62; page 63; page 64.*

BOB CLEMENZ—*pages 40-41; pages 56-57.*

VIC PASCHAL—*page 21.*

ROBERT POLLOCK—*page 18; page 30; page 42; page 58.*

JERRY SIEVE—*page 23; page 26; page 28; page 31; page 45; page 50.*

**Color Separations
by
Universal Color
Beaverton, Oregon**

Beautiful America Publishing Company

The nation's foremost publisher of quality color photography

Current Books

Alaska	Maryland	Oregon Coast
Arizona	Massachusetts	Oregon Country
Boston	Michigan	Pennsylvania
British Columbia	Michigan Country	Philadelphia
California	Michigan Waters	Pittsburgh
California Coast	Minnesota	Portland, Oregon
California Desert	Missouri	San Diego
California Missions	Montana	San Francisco
California Mountains	Monterey Peninsula	San Juan Islands
Chicago	Mt. Hood, Oregon	Seattle
Colorado Country	New Hampshire	Southern California
Dallas	New Jersey	Texas
Delaware	New Mexico	Utah
Florida	New York	Utah Country
Georgia	Northern California	Vancouver U.S.A.
Hawaii	Northern Nevada	Vermont
Idaho	North Carolina	Virginia
Illinois	North Idaho	Washington
Iowa	Oahu	Washington, D.C.
Las Vegas	Ohio	Wisconsin
Los Angeles	Oklahoma	Wyoming
Maine	Orange County	Yosemite National Park
Manhattan	Oregon	

Forthcoming Books

Alabama	Kansas	Phoenix
Arkansas	Kauai	Rhode Island
Baltimore	Kentucky	Rocky Mountains
Connecticut	Maui	South Carolina
Denver	Mississippi	South Dakota
Detroit	New England	Tennessee
The Great Lakes	North Dakota	Washington Adventures
Houston	Oregon Adventures	West Virginia
Indiana	Pacific Coast	

Large Format, Hardbound Books

Beautiful America	Glory of Nature's Form	Volcanoes of the West
Beauty of California	Lewis & Clark Country	Western Impressions
	Los Angeles 200 Years	

Special Interest Books

Beauty of America	Desert Wildflowers, N. America	Pacific Coast Wildflowers
California Adventures	Mt. St. Helens, Volcano	Volcano, Mt. St. Helens

Complete Product Catalog Available

Colorado

State Flower: *Rocky Mountain Columbine*
State Nickname: *Centennial State*
State Bird: *Lark Bunting*
State Animal: *Rocky Mountain Bighorn Sheep*
State Motto: *Nothing Without Providence*

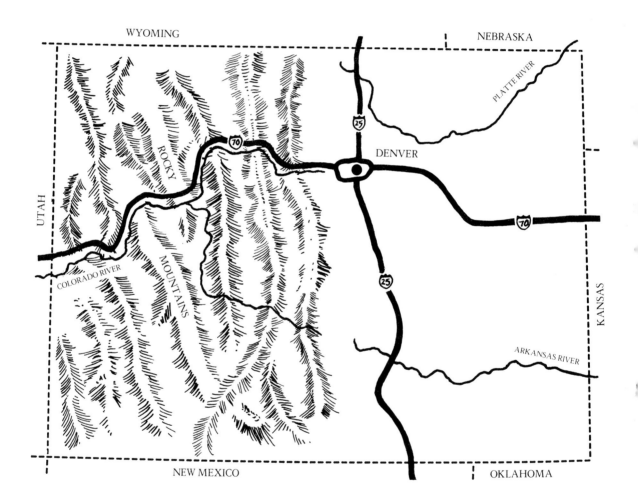